Mel Bay Presents

DALE MILLER
COUNTRY BLUES & RAGTIME
GUITAR STYLES

C000044037

Published in conjunction with Fantasy/Kicking Mule Records

Visit us on the Web at www.melbay.com — E-mail us at email@melbay.com

Table of Contents

About the Author

Dale Miller is a fingerstyle guitarist living in Berkeley, California. He is part owner of Noe Valley Music, a guitar shop in San Francisco. In addition to working behind the counter at his store and playing the occasional gig, Miller is a regular contributor to *Acoustic Guitar Magazine,* teaches private guitar lessons, and is a computer consultant and trouble shooter for a San Francisco law firm.

Miller recorded three critically acclaimed solo-guitar records in the 1970s for *Kicking Mule Records.* The first of these, *Fingerpicking Rags and Other Delights,* has just been re-released on Fantasy Records. In 1994 Miller released a CD/cassette entitled *Both of Me,* featuring overdubbed fingerstyle/slide duets of jazz standards which was extremely well received by critics.

Country Blues and Ragtime Guitar Styles is an update of a Kicking Mule Records book/tape project from 1989.

Photo © Barbara S. Brundage

How to Use This Book

The goal of this book is to give you a basic vocabulary of country blues and ragtime-guitar licks. It offers fourteen original acoustic-guitar solos inspired by the playing of the masters of the style who recorded in the late 1920s and early 1930s.

To get started you should know at least all the first-position chords, have enough control of your right-hand fingers to consistently hit a given string with a given finger, and have some experience with keeping a steady bass going with your right-hand thumb. From a theory point of view you should know what "twelve-barre blues" means and have some knowledge of intervals.

Keep in mind that while the solo-guitar format allows you to hear the licks clearly and is appealing to listen to in its own right, traditionally country blues entertainers have been and continue to be singer/guitarists who brilliantly coordinate voice and guitar.

Don't feel you have to work through this book cover-to-cover. Feel free to learn the tunes or even licks in any order, to get sidetracked investigating a given artist or style, or to simply stop for a couple of weeks and do some jamming and playing by ear. Be patient. It takes years of listening, practicing, performing, and just living to play with anywhere near the confidence, spontaneity, and soul of old masters such as Son House, Mississippi John Hurt, Memphis Minnie, Skip James, Robert Johnson, Mance Lipscomb and Charley Patton or current practitioners like Alvin Youngblood Hart, Catfish Keith, Taj Mahal, and John Hammond.

Guitars, Fingernails, Etc.

All country blues pickers use steel-string guitars, and most prefer instruments with smaller and narrower bodies than the dreadnought size which has become the defacto standard. I use a Martin 00016, which has a sweet tone that suits my style, and a National Style O, which has a fat midrangy sound that's great for slide. You can get started on any six-string guitar (or 12 string for that matter)—nylon, electric, whatever.

I play with my bare fingers and short (though existent) nails. This is fairly common among blues pickers past and present. The two other common right hand approaches are thumb pick and bare fingers and thumb and finger picks (I've never seen anyone play with bare thumb and finger picks). Some revivalists will use or not use picks, changing from tune to tune, depending on whom they are trying to emulate. If you're an accomplished flatpicker you could incorporate these licks into your style by using the flatpick as your "thumb" and picking with the middle and ring fingers.

Many traditional blues pickers played with only the right-hand thumb and index finger. Today more probably use the thumb and two fingers. This is what I do, though I will add the ring and/or pinky for rippling through a four- or five-note chord. Anchoring the right hand on the face of the guitar with the ring finger and/or pinky is probably more common than not among blues pickers, though I personally prefer not to.

◈ Roots and History of Blues ◈

The answer to the question "What is the Blues?" depends on whom you're asking. A musician might talk about the blues progression, pentatonic scales, flatted sevenths, minor thirds, and improvisation. A folklorist might talk about the blending of African and European cultures, the three-verse song form of the last century, and the symbolic and hidden meaning of blues lyrics. An African-American intellectual might tell you it represents a feeling that goes down to the very roots of being black in American. A fan might say, "I'm not sure, but I know them when I hear them." Increasingly, Madison Avenue types are saying, "they're a good way to sell jeans or cars or beer or whatever."

Most scholars now agree the blues began as a distinct form around the turn of the century with the first generation of African-Americans to come to maturity after the abolition of slavery. They were going through social changes, and cheap guitars, available from the Sears Catalog and other sources, were beginning to rival banjos and fiddles as instruments of choice in rural areas.

The first written record of blues we have is from W.C. Handy, an educated middle-class African-American, who accepted a commission as band director of the Knights of Pythias Band in Clarksdale, Mississippi in the heart of the delta in 1903. He went there with the typical prejudice of the educated elite against "primitive" music, but he became a convert on a lonely night in Tutwieler. The train was nine hours late and Handy fell asleep outdoors at the station. He was awakened in the middle of the night to the sound of a man in ragged clothes fretting a Sears guitar with a knife blade and singing "Goin' Where the Southern cross the Dog." The lonely bluesman repeated the line three times, answering with the slide. Handy asked the man what the lyrics meant and was told that the "Southern" meant the Southern Railroad and the "Dog" meant the Yellow Dog or Yazoo Railroad. Fittingly, the first blues notated was about a crossroads.

Handy was impressed and continued to listen to this kind of music as he toured with his band. He went on to fame as the composer of many famous tunes such as "St. Louis Blues." As the first person with a traditional education to get into blues he became known as "The Father of the Blues." Today the most prestigious blues awards are called the Handys, and his statue is on legendary Beale Street in Memphis, Tennessee.

But where did blues come from? The logical starting point is Africa. Many of the slaves came from an area of great musical and cultural traditions called by folklorists Senegambia (where the countries of Senegal and Gambia are today). The principal tribes of this area were and are the Bambara, Huasa, Wolof, and Mandigo (of Kunta Kinte fame). Stringed instruments were very common among these tribes including the kora, godgye, dyulu, and hallam. The hallam is especially interesting. This lute-like instrument had an animal skin head and five strings including a high drone string on the "bass end." This is, of course, the exact set up of the banjo. The influence of stringed instruments on the development of American music became even more important when the Black Codes were passed after bloody uprisings in Haiti and elsewhere. These laws outlawed the playing of drums and flutes which white slave owners correctly felt were powerful forms of communication.

Though it's hard to hear much similarity between blues and traditional African music, there is a lot in the African culture that influenced the way blues performers saw themselves and were seen by their audience. Most African religion at the time of the slave trade before the advance of Islam was pantheistic. The Africans believed gods such as Legba (God of the crossroads) were everywhere and in everything. They believed in magic, medicine men (and women), and shamans. Among these shamans were the Griot singers who sang historical and genealogical records. They were believed to have great mystical power and were respected and even feared. They, like many members of tribal societies, had secret names they never revealed, since to know the someone's true name was to have power over him.

Many of these cultural aspects carried over into the blues world. Blues performers were thought to be in league with the Devil and often adopted stage names such as "The Devil's Son In Law," "Howlin' Wolf," "Muddy Waters," "The Mississippi Mudder," and "The Masked Marvel." They sang about and used secret herbs, magic potions and charms like mojos. Talk of musicians selling their souls to the Devil was common and taken seriously.

The earliest African-American music in the New World was probably the work song. Obviously work was the reason for slavery, and just as obviously most folks work better while singing. Work songs were sung to the rhythm of the falling hammer or axe and were improvised about what was happening at the time. Usually phrases were stated and repeated as in blues.

Spirituals were also sung from early on. The Black Codes banned large secular gatherings of African-Americans, but church membership and attendance were usually encouraged as a way of shifting the focus of slaves away from the unfairness of their present life to the promise of the afterlife. Inevitably, many African practices crept into the services such as being possessed by spirits, speaking in tongues, and the use of poisonous snakes. The strong tradition of black gospel music was born—what Dr. King and others of his generation called "Negro Spirituals." As in blues there was plenty of room for singers to improvise within the form.

Throughout American history there has been a constant battle between blues and gospel for the soul of many African-Americans. Son House, Robert Wilkens, Rube Lacy, and many others went back and forth between the religious and secular worlds as we've seen Little Richard and others do later on. The great slide guitarist Blind Willie Johnson and other musicians have used the techniques covered in this book to play only gospel music. Anyone my age remembers the influence of black gospel in the creation of soul music and on the civil rights movement in the 1950s and 1960s.

Slaves arrived with no baggage or even clothes, but they immediately began to adapt their music to Western instruments such as the fiddle and to reconstruct their own instruments. The banjo, adapted from the Senegambian hallam, took the world by storm in the Nineteenth Century. White and some black entertainers dressed in blackface and toured in minstrel shows, cracking stupid jokes and performing so called "coon" songs such as the notorious "Jump Jim Crow." This style continued into the Twentieth Century. What could be more American than a poor Jewish immigrant adapting an Anglo-Saxon name, blackening his face, and singing about Dixie to international audiences. That's the story of Al Jolson, the self-styled "World's Greatest Entertainer."

One of the most exciting aspects of black music to white ears was syncopation, where notes fell slightly off the beat. This "ragged" rhythm became more formalized in an extremely popular musical style that developed among black folks after slavery. As bands played syncopated music, couples strutted up and down in front of a crowd. A cake was awarded to the couple with the best outfit and demeanor. This formalized event and musical style became known as the Cakewalk. Ragtime grew from this, spurred by the great Scott Joplin. He was a classically trained musician who composed complex, formal four-movement works that were highly syncopated. He took himself and his music very seriously and sought respect from the established musical community. He even composed an opera which is still performed occasionally. His works were huge hits in sheet music sales from the 1890s well into the Twentieth Century. Ragtime's popularity was on the wane when the recording of country blues began in the mid to late 1920s, but many of the early country blues stars, though not attempting to recreate the complex four-movement works of Joplin, used ragtime syncopation and chord progressions in their playing.

Another important tradition we should discuss as a precursor to blues is that of the songster. From the days of the ancient Greeks and probably before, right up until the rise of mass literacy and mass media, singers have been our story tellers. The arrival of a songster was an exciting event in any ancient village—classical Greek, mediaeval European, or ancient African. The Provencal troubadours, the Greek poet Homer, and the African Griots are all part of this tradition. Many early bluesmen sang straight ahead ballads such as "Stagger Lee," "The Titanic," "Frankie and Johnny," and "John Henry" as well as blues ballads such as "High Water Everywhere" and "Dry Spell Blues."

Perhaps the first blues recorded was by Mamie Smith with the Rega Orchestra in August of 1920. It was a composed "city" blues in the W.C. Handy tradition with big band accompaniment. What John Lee Hooker and others call "deep blues" wasn't recorded until 1926 when the invention of electronic recording made it possible to record softer instruments like guitars, and to carry recording equipment in the trunk of a car. Soon Blind Lemon Jefferson, Blind Blake, Charley Patton, Son House, Memphis Minnie, Tampa Red and others were recording stars with fans wherever African-Americans lived.

This golden age lasted into the mid to late 1930s. It was slowed by the depression and finally all but killed with wartime restrictions on the materials used for recordings. After the war blues went electric and continued to grow and evolve in different ways. In the meantime college-educated white record collectors began to discover the great 78s recorded by the early acoustic blues players. By the late 1950s a new generation was learning to play some of the tunes from these records. In the early 1960s, some of the more curious of these young fans started searching out folks like Reverend Gary Davis, Mississippi John Hurt, Bukka White, Lightnin' Hopkins, Skip James, and Mance Lipscomb. Many of these rediscovered heroes enjoyed a second (or first in the case of Lipscomb) recording and performing career on the folk circuit.

Today, the tradition of country blues lives on with many outstanding revivalists touring and recording and many great performances by the singer/guitarists from the 1920s and 1930s available on CD, cassette, and even video tape.

Tampa Red

Born Hudson Woodbridge in Smithville, Georgia in 1903, Red became a studio musician in Atlanta and Chicago. He was very light skinned and had red hair. He played slide in open E style tuning and often dueted with pianist Thomas A. "Georgia Tom" Dorsey, who became one of gospel music's biggest stars. Red's style was more melodic than chordal, and he really exploited the sustain and fat tone of his National guitar.

The first time through this composition while in the tonic E chord I play a boogie - woogie bass line under mostly arpeggiated open-string licks in the treble. This technique is not from Red, but I worked it out after learning his "Boogie Woogie Dance" as a contrast to the fat ringing licks he uses. These licks have become the variation or "break" in this tune. In this tuning the IV (A) and V7 (B7) chords are fingered like this.

If you like to sing try out a rock 'n' roll or jump blues chestnut like "Whole Lot a Shakin' Goin' On" or "Shake, Rattle and Roll" with the boogie-woogie bass section.

Other traditional slide players who used this tuning include Blind Willie Johnson and Robert Johnson.

Tampa Red

E tuning = E B E G♯ B E

Dale Miller

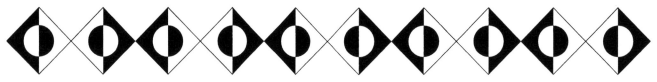

Your Standard Robert Johnson

It's fitting that one of Johnson's greatest hits was "Crossroads Blues," since he was such a pivotal figure between the acoustic blues of Son House, Charley Patton, and other delta players and the postwar electric sounds of Muddy Waters, Jimmy Reed, and Elmore James.

Johnson's life was shrouded in mystery until researchers figured out he had changed his name after his birth. Now most scholars agree he was born Robert Spencer in 1911 in Hazelhurst, Mississippi. As a youngster Johnson hung out with Son House and Willie Brown, pestering them for guitar licks and attempting to accompany them on harmonica. House remembers him as being not particularly good. But Johnson disappeared for a couple of years and returned playing so well House was convinced he had sold his soul to the devil.

When Johnson recorded a few years later in 1937 he laid down some of the finest blues tracks in history, proving equally brilliant at guitar playing, singing, and song writing. He was lined up to play John Hammond's famous Spirituals to Swing concert in 1938 when he was poisoned by a jealous husband. He was only twenty-six or twenty-seven years old. A few years ago a deluxe CD re-release of Johnson's complete works became a surprise best-seller and helped usher in an acoustic blues revival that continues today.

This tune features many of Johnson's favorite licks in the key of A which he used for tunes such as "Kindhearted Woman Blues." I've also borrowed a few licks from Willie Brown's "Mississippi Blues." The two tunes mesh nicely as the D9th triplet lick of Brown's flows into the Robert Johnson style turnaround with the pinky anchored at the fifth fret while the other fingers execute a descending chromatic bass line on the fifth string. Much of the overall feel of this piece was inspired by the slow blues duets of pianist Leroy Carr and guitarist Scrapper Blackwell. The licks up the neck that begin the piece after the turnaround are all executed off of a first position D7 type chord moved up the neck. When the piece comes back to the tonic A7 I use this version of a Robert Johnson voicing that I've altered to allow for the index finger to sneak in behind the chord and play the G natural on the first string. The index finger comes on and off the first string and the other three fingers move the chord down a fret and back up as the tablature shows.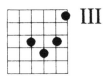

When playing tunes inspired by Johnson and other delta players I've opted to even out the timing and play strict 4/4 measures. This is not necessarily an improvement, but certainly makes jamming with other musicians easier. Many old blues players would extend a measure by a beat or two and/or add an extra measure or two to create tension and drama, often changing from verse to verse. It's another sort of improvisation.

As with the Tampa Red piece, I play a steady thumping bass unlike Johnson who had the amazing ability to trick listeners' minds into hearing bass lines that weren't there by sneaking back and forth from the bass to the treble strings. I learned the steady bass style early on from listening to and observing the playing of folks like Mississippi John Hurt and Mance Lipscomb. As I got into other blues artists I tended to adapt their licks into the steady bass style.

Your Standard Robert Johnson

Capo II—true key is B

Dale Miller

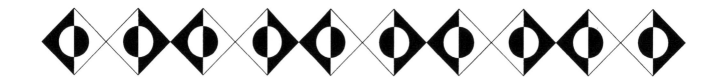

Texas Style Blues

E is probably the most organic blues key especially for this steady bass Texas style. The root note is on the open sixth string and you can easily hammer from a minor to a major third (third string open to third string/first fret) and add the flatted seventh (second string/third fret).

I had the good fortune to meet and hear Mance Lipscomb and Lightnin' Hopkins, two of the greatest Texas blues pickers, while I was a student at the University of Texas in the mid 1960s. The music scene in Austin at that time was much smaller than today's. Anyone could get on stage at the Id Coffeehouse, and you could dance to the psychedelic Thirteenth-Floor Elevators at the Eleventh Door. I had a nodding acquaintance with cartoonist Gilbert Shelton and the not-yet-famous Janis Joplin and met novelist Billy Lee Bramer, but my biggest thrill was sharing a half-pint bottle of cheap bourbon as part of a five person circle including washboard player Cleveland Chenier and Hopkins at a party.

Hopkins was a guy who liked to party and was a fabulous blues stylist, but Lipscomb was the better guitar player whose best asset was his great thumb technique. He'd keep thumping out a hypnotic powerful bass drone under inventive treble licks, playing confidently in all the common finger style guitar keys (C, G, D, A, and E). Hopkins stuck closer to blues and favored the key of E above all others.

Both guitarists liked to move up to play licks in the second position. I do a lot of that in this piece and in others in this package. I'll keep the bass thumping, slide my second finger on the G string up to the fourth fret and play some or all the notes in this pyramid shape.

I also use the same Robert Johnson A chord voicing as "Your Standard Robert Johnson." It's pretty obvious, really, but taking a lick from an A blues and using it in an E blues is a simple way to expand your vocabulary of blues licks.

Texas Style Blues

Dale Miller

15

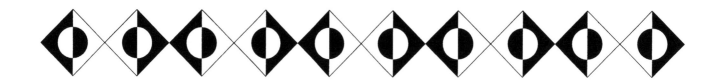

Dale's Boogie Blues

The feel of this tune is reminiscent of the playing of Texas blues stylist and songster Mance Lipscomb, who was a major influence of mine as I discussed in the intro to the last tune. Lipscomb was the same age as folks like Mississippi John Hurt, Skip James, and Bukka White but had no professional career in the 1920s and 1930s. He lived as a share cropper in Navasota, Texas until his discovery by Chris Strachwitz of Arhoolie Records in the 1960s. He was a professional musician for the last ten years of his life, and no early bluesman played better or put on a more impressive show. With no evidence to the contrary, it's comforting for middle-aged guitarists like myself to think that Lipscomb slowly improved his whole life and played his best music in his sixties and seventies.

Notice how adding the different bass note at the end of the measures in A to an otherwise monotonic bass line creates a bit of interest and drive. This note not only complicates the bass line but becomes part of the melody line as well. "The John Hurt Riff" uses the same bass line in a different key and tuning.

The turnaround is from the playing of Robert Johnson and is one I use all the time for blues in this key. On a slow blues I'll give it a more triplet feel. On the recurring slide lick move up the entire 2/3 barre A chord and have the pinky ready to get that high A note. For the D9 I use the following simple fingering with my thumb wrapped over the back of the neck to get the low F♯.

D9th

The variations are played with the index finger playing a 2/3 barre on the second fret. These licks are easier to play and work even better in the key of G, by the way, with the nut taking the place of the barre.

I decided to capo at the fourth fret on this tune for a brighter sound.

Dale's Boogie Blues

Capo IV—true key is C#

Dale Miller

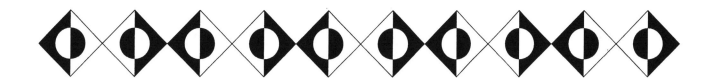

Blind Blake's Like This

Blake was a brilliant guitar stylist who was the second biggest seller behind Blind Lemon Jefferson in the 1920s. Originally from Florida, he became a studio musician in Chicago and Atlanta. Blake's playing is very uptown and disciplined with regular 4/4 measures and ragtime chord progressions. His style is extremely crisp and accurate with a thumb that's amazingly quick and syncopated. In print advertisements for his records the company would often accurately mention Blake's "piano-sounding guitar."

On a tune like this Blake would sing and play the A section various times with variations, but here I've added a B section that is typical for this chord progression and gives the tune the added interest I feel it needed to work as a guitar solo. The couple of tunes by Blake's this is close to are "That'll Never Happen No More" and "Too Tight Rag." The turnaround features the three chords pictured below resolving to a standard G. Notice the great counter motion—the top string stays put, the second string moves up, and the bass descends chromatically in a classic blues line (flat 7, 6, flat 6, 5). One way of looking at this turnaround is that it's a more complicated variation of the Robert Johnson A turnaround I discussed in the intro to "Your Standard Robert Johnson."

G/F

C/E

E♭7

Blind Blake's Like This

Capo IV—true key is B

Dale Miller

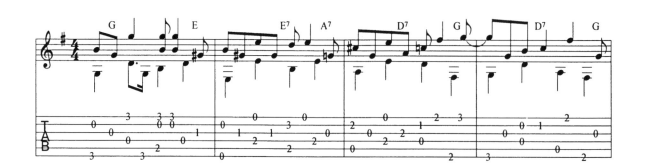

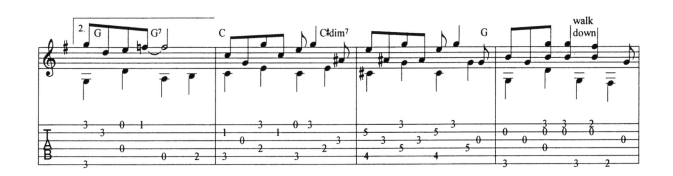

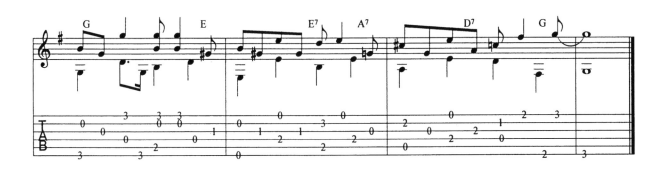

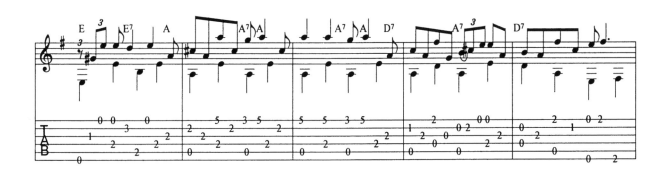

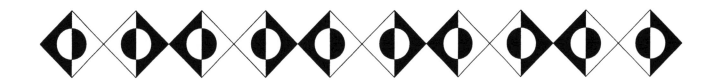

Skip James Style

Nehemiah "Skip" James' blues are among the deepest and most unique on record. He was born in Bentonia, Mississippi in 1903 and spent his life as a musician, gambler, and bootlegger. A recent biography of James paints him as a complex, dark, depressed, and even evil personality, a characterization that isn't hard to believe when you listen to his powerful music.

James played almost exclusively in an open D minor style tuning [Root, V, Root, minor 3rd, V, Root] using a subtle three-finger picking style. He'd often tune below D to give his guitar an especially muddy, menacing sound. In a very effective contrast, he'd sing in a haunting, mysterious falsetto, usually about death and the dark side with lyrics such as, "When your knee bones get to achin', and your body's gettin' cold, you know you're gettin' ready for the Cypress Grove."

The intro to the following tune is from James' "Devil Got My Woman" and the first time through is from "Hard Time Killin' Floor." After that I play the melody to "Killin' Floor" with variations using slide on the treble strings, a technique not used by James, and a lick from his "Cypress Grove." For the intro use a standard D7 type chord up a couple of frets and then bring it down as the music shows. For the rest of the song just play the notes as they come.

One advantage of this tuning is that all the licks you know on the first three strings in the key of E work well. That run from "Cypress Grove," for example, uses the second position just as "Texas Blues" does, only here it falls in the key of D because you've tuned down.

Skip James Style

Open D minor tuning—D A D F A D

Dale Miller

slide notes

play these notes with fingers

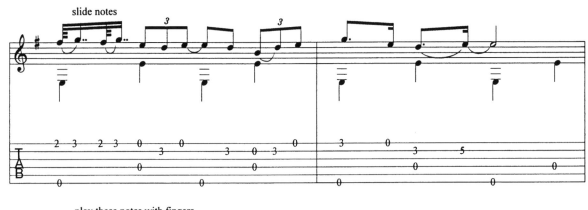

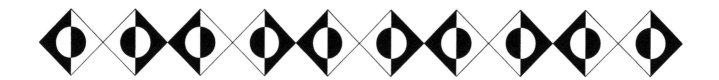

The John Hurt Riff

For me the greatest thing about Mississippi John Hurt was his ability to find riffs that sound complicated but are relatively easy to execute. "Frankie and Albert," which he played in an open G type tuning (V, Root, V, Root, major 3rd, V), contains some examples. I've taken the main riff from that song and built it into a twelve-barre blues that rocks along quite well and makes a great accompaniment for rock 'n' roll hits. In the variation I play another important riff from "Frankie" where Hurt jumped up and grabbed the first string/fifth fret note and let it ring out over a cute moving bass line. The steady alternating bass of this tune is typical of all his playing.

This great song, more often called "Frankie and Johnny," was, along with "Stagger Lee" and "Louis Collins," one of the murder ballads Hurt would perform. Even though Frankie, Louis, and Stagger were definitely bad boys who blasted away with their six shooters at the least provocation and killed a bunch of folks, Hurt made it all sound kind of cute and innocent with his mellow voice, impish smile, and relaxed demeanor. When the Jim Kweskin Jug Band introduced him as "Mister Hippie John Hurt" at the Newport Folk Festival in 1964 with your author in attendance, they were making one of the all time great true puns we musicians love to hear.

Hurt was from Avalon, Mississippi which is in the hill country, an area of small farms to the east of the delta. While the socioeconomic structure of the delta is rich whites owning large plantations worked by dirt poor black sharecroppers, that of the hill country is more egalitarian with black and white families both owning small plots of land and working hard for themselves. Not surprisingly, Hurt's music in many ways is closer to that of early white fingerpickers like Sam Magee and Ike Everly than the deep delta sounds of folks like James, Patton, and Johnson. He was probably the most successful of the blues artists rediscovered in the 1960s. For me personally, as a folky in that decade, Hurt was the perfect bridge from the sweet styles of Peter, Paul, and Mary to the dark, powerful blues of James and Patton in my listening and development as a guitarist.

The John Hurt Riff

Open A tuning—E B E G♯ B E

Dale Miller

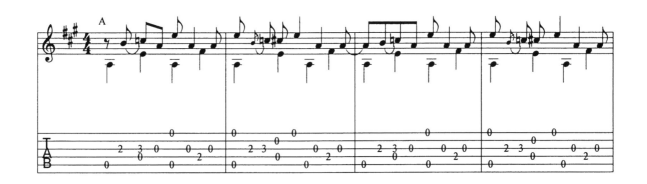

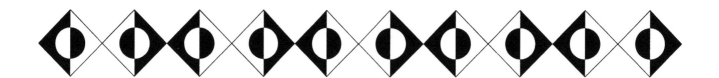

Let's Drop D Blues

This tune isn't tied closely to any one particular artist or tune, at least consciously. It's probably closest to William Moore's "Ragtime Millionaire" and has some riffs close to those of Tommy Johnson's playing in this tuning.

I do some string snapping in this piece which was and continues to be a common technique for country blues. To snap you pick up a string with your thumb or finger, pull it up and let go so it pops back against the fretboard. The bridge has this sweet A9th voicing up at the sixth fret that's used in Willie Brown's "Mississippi Blues," though in that tune and this one you can skip the fourth string/seventh-fret note if you like.

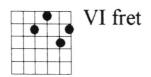 VI fret

Let's Drop D Blues

Drop low E string to D

Dale Miller

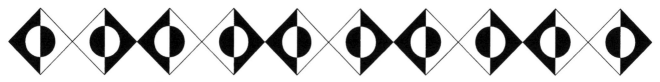

Johnson Meets Patton

You could add the name of Willie Brown to the above two names as well. This tune features some slow soulful blues licks in the key of E. It has the feel of and borrows some licks from Patton's "Pony Blues," Johnson's "Lonesome Home Blues" (which I believe featured Ishman Bracy on guitar), and Brown's "M and O Blues." Unlike those guys I keep a steady bass going and stick to steady 4/4 measures. As with most of the tunes in this package I'm also playing softer. This certainly doesn't mean I've improved things in any way, I've just adapted their licks to my technique and background.

Patton was the first delta bluesman to record. He was born in the country between Vicksburg and Jackson, Mississippi in 1891. His grandfather was a white man legally married to Patton's Indian/White grandmother. Since his mother's side of the family had many Indian members, Patton was actually more Indian than African in his genealogical makeup, but was certainly black from a social point of view. He spent most of his adult life at Dockery's plantation, near Cleveland on the Sunflower River where his family moved in 1901. Dockery ran a relatively easy going plantation and Patton felt comfortable there. He learned guitar from Henry Sloan, a first generation bluesman who never recorded. There is a chance Sloan was the man W.C. Handy heard playing guitar at the Tutwieler train station.

Patton recorded in 1928 and became the most famous musician in the area. He roamed all over the delta and was able to make a very comfortable living as a professional musician and recording star. He was a great showman, and really lived the blues lifestyle of womanizing and drinking.

Tommy Johnson was perhaps the leading figure of the rich blues scene around Jackson, Mississippi. He was born on the George Miller plantation a few miles south of Jackson near the township of Terry on the Illinois Central Railroad line in 1896. He learned to play guitar from his older brother LeDell. At a very young age he ran away from home with an older woman and met up with Patton in Drew, Mississippi. He later returned to Drew and began playing professionally. Charley McCoy, Memphis Minnie's brother-in-law and member of the Mississippi Sheiks, often played second guitar behind Johnson in a single string, mandolin-like style. Johnson had a rich baritone voice with a fabulous falsetto that is one of the best in blues history. One of his compositions was "Canned Heat Blues," which became the name of a sixties rock band that had a number one hit called "Going' Up the Country," featuring a flute break from Henry Thomas' "Bull Doze Blues." Canned heat was the liquid you get by straining Sterno through a napkin, a favorite beverage of poor folks in prohibition days.

The E chord up the neck in this song is a useful and cool one.

The lick you play is weird it use because the second-string note is higher than the open-first string which sort of short circuits your brain until you get used to it.

I'm playing an interesting guitar on this cut. It's a cheap 1950s Stella painted jet black with a Seymour Duncan "Jeff Beck" pickup mounted in the sound hole with a wire coat hanger. This guitar, played through a cheap Gorilla amp, proved to have a great sound for this tune. Thanks to my friend Dennis White for the loan.

Johnson Meets Patton

Dale Miller

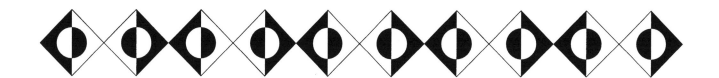

Texas Rag

The key of C is great for ragtime style blues like this one that feature a lot of syncopation and harmonic restlessness. While keys like E and A make playing droning bass lines easy, C makes it easy to play moving bass lines and chord progressions that back pedal through the circle of fifths. Some old blues tunes this is related to are Blind Blake's "Diddie Wa Diddie" and Big Bill Broonzy's "Long Tall Mama." Much of the playing of Blind Boy Fuller sounds like this as well.

The hardest part of this piece is the double hammer into the F chord, a trick I figured out organically one day. I fret the fourth-string note with my third finger and the low sixth-string note with my thumb up over the neck and then start the hammer, first coming down with the entire part of my index finger above the second joint for a three-string barre and then following with my second finger on the second fret. When I finish I'm in the F chord.

As with most ragtime playing I'm making the chord changes on the off beat before the first or third beat of a measure. The substitution of a II V I chord progression for the normal blues V IV I change is another common technique in ragtime blues picking.

Texas Rag

Capo II—true key is D

Dale Miller

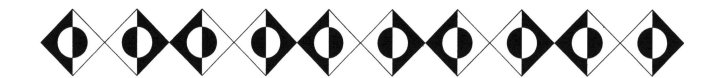

Tommy Johnson Alone

I adapted the starting lick for this tune from the classic Jimmy Reed riff he used for all his hits, though played in the key of A or E. This lick has been borrowed by rock 'n' rollers where it's often played with a barred A style chord. Here I've slowed it way down and added the droning alternating bass for a murky, delta-like sound. The lick in G is quite close to Johnson's in "Canned Heat Blues," though I keep the bass going and brush up with my fingers while Johnson gets into a strumming thing.

The first variation is almost note for note what Johnson plays in "Canned Heat," while the second variation is almost note for note from Blind Blake's "Chump Man Blues," a much faster and brighter ragtime-style blues. It's a valuable lesson to keep in mind—often by changing the tempo and feel of a lick you redefine it even without changing the notes.

I use a lot of string snapping on this tune and often brush a note in a purposely "sloppy" style rather than trying to pluck it cleanly as I would on a "ragtimey" tune. I have to confess that I started goofing around with this tune after listening to a CD by the rock group *The Jesus and Mary Chain,* who play a very dark, ponderous, muddy, hypnotic, and emotional style of rock on highly distorted electric guitars. I have a feeling I'd walk out of a live performance by this group, but luckily I can adjust the volume of the record for my middle-aged ears.

Tommy Johnson Alone

Dale Miller

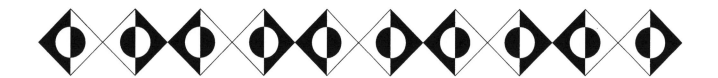

Robert Johnson in Open G

This tune's starting lick is a great A7-A6 change of Johnson's that really sets a great groove.

The slide lick up the neck is from "Come Into My Kitchen" where he says "hear the wind cryin.'"

Again I've kept a steady bass going and evened out the song to strict 4/4 time and a twelve-barre format.

One of Johnson's greatest strengths was his ability to mold a three-minute song with an intro, outro, well thought out breaks and lyrics composed to fit into the framework. He obviously thought in terms of creating something to fit on the side of a record unlike Charley Patton, Son House, and others whose sides often featured fade-ins and fade-outs on songs that probably went on for ten or more minutes when played at a "Juke Joint." He was very modern in this way and he has been a huge influence on rock 'n' rollers.

Robert Johnson in Open G

Tuning = D G D G B D

Dale Miller

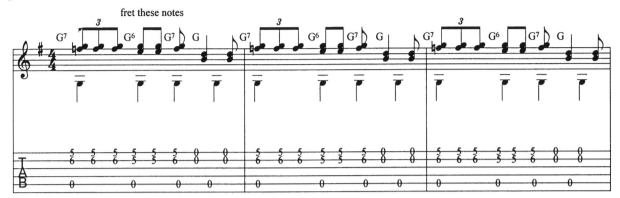

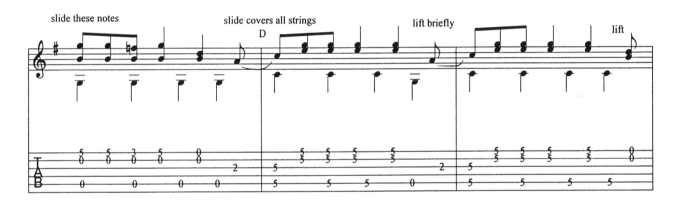

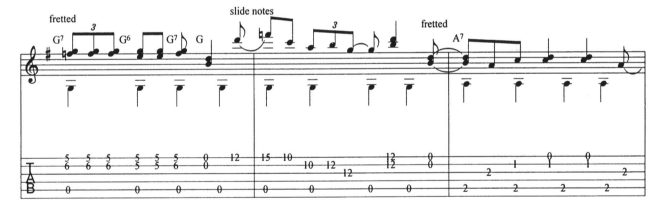

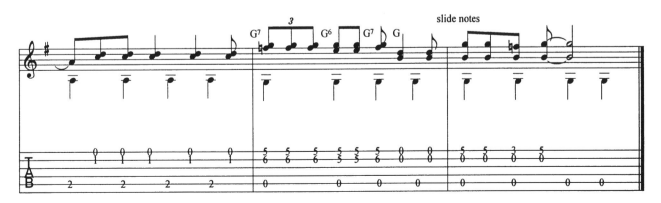

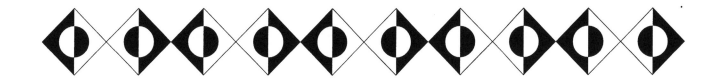

Dale's Ragtime Blues

In many ways this tune is the most uniquely my own of all in this package. I worked out a lot of these moving bass techniques on long lonely evenings in South America before returning to discover others had been doing similar things back in the States. The tune begins as a straight twelve-barre blues and then back pedals through the Circle of Fifths in the ninth and tenth measures before returning to a blues format for a turnaround in the last two measures. It's important to never lift a finger when you don't have to. The bass and treble lines need to sound separate for this tune to work.

As you can hear I'm all over the map in the variations to this tune.

Circle of Fifths

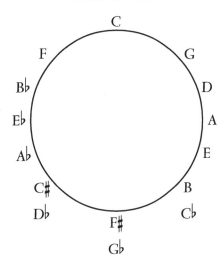

Dale's Ragtime Blues

Capo II—true key is A

Dale Miller

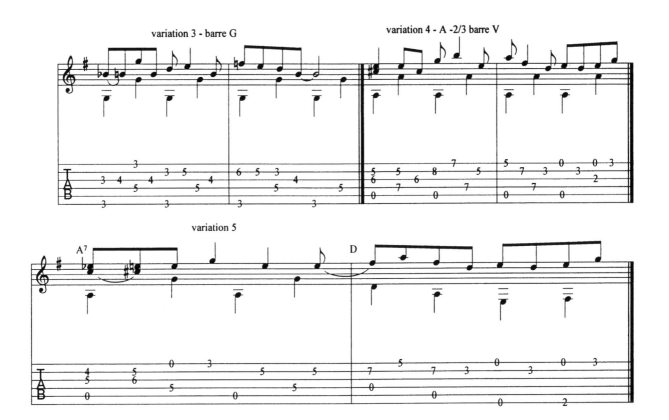

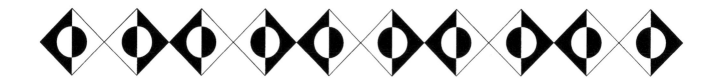

Son House Style

House was one of many blues players who spent much of his life in torment, ping-ponging between the sinful lifestyle of Juke Joints, casual sex, drinking, and gambling and the solid, respectable world of the church. He was born in Coahama County, Mississippi in 1902. He was a very religious youngster and had his own church by the age of twenty. At that time he had a passionate affair with an older woman and ran away with her. He later returned and began to play guitar, learning first from James McCoy and then Rube Lacy. He developed his own style, one of the most dynamic and influential in the delta, which featured a lot of slide work, rhythmic complexity, and virtually no true chord changes. His attack, like most blues pickers of his generation, was extremely strong and his voice carried great power and conviction.

In 1928 House was convicted of manslaughter and sent the notorious Parchman Farm Prison. After a couple of years there and a subsequent pardon he headed north to Lula where he met Charley Patton and Willie Brown. They became friends and Patton helped House get a recording session. House went on to record six sides which became collectors items among blues aficionados.

House was rediscovered in the 1960s and went on to a second career. He lived to a very old age and died in 1988.

This tune is mostly a reworking of House's "Dry Spell Blues." As with most delta blues I've "straightened" it out quite a bit and added some other licks. This is one of the few guitar tunes played entirely with slide and no fretted notes.

Photo by Dale Miller

Son House Style

Open A tuning—E A E A C♯ E

Dale Miller